Cheetahs

NATURE'S PREDATORS

Nathan Aaseng

KidHaven Press, an imprint of Greenhaven Press,
P.O. Box 289009, San Diego, CA 92198-9009

Library of Congress Cataloging-in-Publication Data

Aaseng, Nathan.
    Cheetahs / by Nathan Aaseng.
        p. cm. —(Nature's Predators)
    Includes bibliographical references (p.   )
    ISBN 0-7377-0700-3 (hardback)
    1. Cheetah—Juvenile literature. [1. Chee-
    tah.] I. Title. II.
    Nature's Predators (San Diego, Calif.)
    QL737.C23 A146 2002
    599.75'9—dc21
    00-012808

Contents

Chapter 1: The Fastest Predator   5

Chapter 2: The Hunt   16

Chapter 3: The Kill   24

Chapter 4: The Hunter Becomes
            the Hunted   34

Glossary   43

For Further Exploration   45

Index   46

Picture Credits   48

Chapter 1

The Fastest Predator

F ew predators can get close to an alert blackbuck. This beautiful antelope with corkscrew horns can run faster than fifty miles per hour. It can also change direction quickly to throw off any beast that gets close.

There is only one meat eater that can chase down an adult blackbuck. That is the cheetah. This slender, spotted cat is the sprint champion of the world. Streaking over the ground at three strides per second, cheetahs have been timed at speeds of nearly seventy miles per hour. This is as fast as a car driving on an interstate highway. Few sights in nature can compare to that of a cheetah racing after a blackbuck in full flight.

Cheetahs are one of the oldest members of the cat family—a group that includes lions, tigers, leopards, and house cats. Their name comes from a word that means "spotted one." Cheetahs are not the only spotted cats; leopards and jaguars also have spots. But cheetahs' spots are smaller and rounder. Cheetahs also have a stripe in the corner of their eye that looks like a teardrop.

Built for Speed

Though they are part of the cat family, cheetahs are very different from leopards, jaguars, and other cats. They are a special type of cat designed for speed. Almost everything about a cheetah's body is geared to help it run down fast prey.

For example, cheetahs carry little weight for an animal of their size. They grow to about the same length as leopards. Most adults are around four feet long, with a few growing to fifty-three inches. But they are slightly taller at the shoulders than leopards and much thinner. They have almost no fat. Their muscles are long and lean to give them power without the weight that would slow them down. Even the cheetah's head and neck are smaller and lighter than those of other big cats. Adult cheetahs can weigh as little as 86 pounds. Seldom do they get as big as 140 pounds.

The cheetah has a very flexible spine and loose joints in its leg and hipbones. This allows it to stretch its legs to a twenty-three-foot stride when it runs. The upper part of the spine has an exceptionally long bone extension that provides an attachment for extra running muscles. A chee-

All cheetahs have distinctive stripes that run from the corner of each eye down to their mouths.

tah has long, thin legs and small, narrow paws. Unlike the other big cats, it cannot fully retract its claws back into the footpad. The claws act something like spikes in track shoes. Along with the ridged toe pads, these give the animal greater grip for running. All of these features allow the cheetah to burst from a standing position to top speed in less than four seconds.

Any creature traveling at the speeds that a cheetah reaches could easily run past a prey that changes direction suddenly. And just as an automobile can overturn when taking a corner at high speed, an animal trying to turn at high speed can easily fall. For the cheetah, the answer to this problem is a very long tail (twenty-six to thirty-three inches). By shifting its tail from one side to the other, a cheetah can keep its balance when making quick changes of direction.

Unlike other big cats, cheetahs have long, lean muscles and small heads.

A cheetah's long and powerful muscles allow it to reach speeds of up to seventy miles per hour.

The Price of Speed

There are some disadvantages in a body built entirely for speed. Cheetahs do not have the strength of other big cats. This means they cannot attack large prey or fight off strong enemies. Many times they are unable to defend their kills from other animals looking for an easy meal.

While the cheetah's claws provide good traction for high-speed sprinting, they are a problem when it comes to climbing. Because they cannot be retracted, the claws are constantly scraping against hard surfaces. They quickly become worn and dull, like those of a dog. Therefore, cheetahs are not much better than dogs at climbing. This means they cannot seek safety from danger in trees the way leopards do.

Just as cars use more gas at high speeds, cheetahs use a great deal of energy in their sprints. Cheetahs must meet this energy demand with a heart that is not well suited for pumping large amounts of blood. Like all other cats, cheetahs have a relatively small heart. They make up for

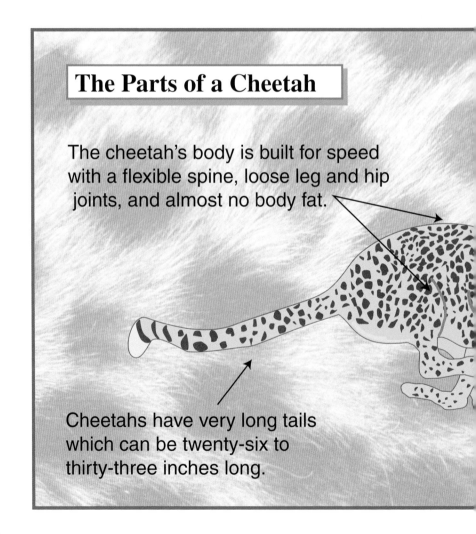

The Parts of a Cheetah

The cheetah's body is built for speed with a flexible spine, loose leg and hip joints, and almost no body fat.

Cheetahs have very long tails which can be twenty-six to thirty-three inches long.

this somewhat by having an extra supply of oxygen in the blood. A bulge in the front of the skull just above the eyes provides a large nasal passage that allows a greater flow of air into the animal's lungs. This allows cheetahs to supply more oxygen to their muscles with each heartbeat.

Having no body fat may make the cheetah lighter and faster, but it also leaves the animal in greater danger of starving. With no fat reserves to

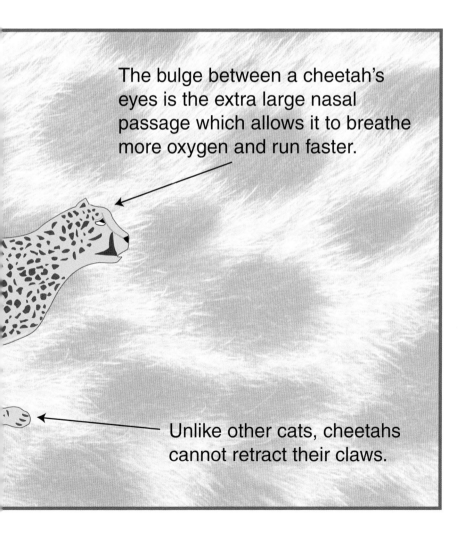

The bulge between a cheetah's eyes is the extra large nasal passage which allows it to breathe more oxygen and run faster.

Unlike other cats, cheetahs cannot retract their claws.

fall back on, a cheetah cannot afford to miss many meals. Unlike leopards, tigers, and lions, which can live on one good-sized animal in a week, cheetahs cannot go more than a few days without making a kill. That can be a particular problem if a cheetah suffers even a minor leg or foot injury. Because they depend so heavily on speed for hunting

Continents of the World

GREENLAND

ASIA

North Pacific Ocean

NORTH AMERICA

North Atlantic Ocean

EUROPE

AFRICA

Pacific Ocean

SOUTH AMERICA

Indian Ocean

South Pacific Ocean

South Atlantic Ocean

AUSTRALIA

success, cheetahs may quickly starve to death if an injury prevents them from running.

Creatures of the Open Plains

Cheetahs would not be able to use their speed to capture prey if they had to weave through trees, plow through dense shrubs, or scramble up steep, rocky hills. For this reason, they hunt best in open, flat plains. Here they can spot prey from a long ways off, creep closer while hidden in grass, and then sprint to catch them.

The open, flat plains where cheetahs thrive are places where rainfall is light and humidity low. Cheetahs are well adapted to such dry conditions. They can go as long as ten days without water. Wildlife researchers have watched them repeatedly pass by water holes without stopping to drink even in the hottest weather.

Cheetahs' main prey prefer the same type of area. The cheetah's favorite prey animal is the Thomson's gazelle. This animal weighs only about forty to sixty pounds full grown—small enough for cheetahs to kill easily. Quick enough to avoid most large predators, these gazelles roam the grasslands in enormous herds. Researchers have counted more than 180,000 in the Serengeti National Park in East Africa. Like the cheetah, they are extremely fast. Their best chance for survival is on the open plain, where they can see predators approaching and can use their speed to escape.

Where Do Cheetahs Live?

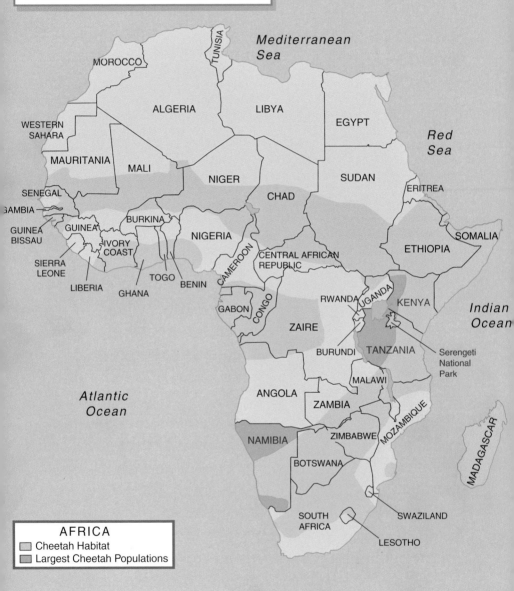

MOROCCO
TUNISIA
Mediterranean Sea
ALGERIA
LIBYA
EGYPT
WESTERN SAHARA
Red Sea
MAURITANIA
MALI
NIGER
SUDAN
ERITREA
SENEGAL
CHAD
GAMBIA
GUINEA BISSAU
GUINEA
BURKINA
NIGERIA
SOMALIA
SIERRA LEONE
IVORY COAST
CAMEROON
CENTRAL AFRICAN REPUBLIC
ETHIOPIA
LIBERIA
TOGO
BENIN
GHANA
GABON
CONGO
RWANDA
UGANDA
KENYA
Indian Ocean
ZAIRE
BURUNDI
TANZANIA
Serengeti National Park
Atlantic Ocean
MALAWI
ANGOLA
ZAMBIA
MOZAMBIQUE
MADAGASCAR
NAMIBIA
ZIMBABWE
BOTSWANA
SWAZILAND
SOUTH AFRICA
LESOTHO

AFRICA
☐ Cheetah Habitat
☐ Largest Cheetah Populations

But an animal that must kill every couple of days cannot afford to be choosy. When a Thomson's gazelle is not available, cheetahs will try for other small hoofed animals such as impalas and springbok. In Namibia, where Thomson's gazelles are rare, their primary prey are the kudu and the warthog. In Iran, where most of their usual prey has vanished, cheetahs have adapted to living off wild sheep. African cheetahs will occasionally go after very young wildebeests, zebras, and even giraffes. Although they do not stalk hares, they easily catch them whenever they flush one out of the brush. They have also been known to eat game birds, aardvarks, jackals, and rats when very hungry.

Animal experts estimate that there are fewer than fifteen thousand wild cheetahs left in the world. They are scattered throughout twenty-six African countries plus Iran, but most of them live in two areas. The largest population lives in the dry grasslands of Namibia in southwestern Africa. This region receives very little rainfall and so has not been farmed heavily and occupied by many people. Despite finding prey more scarce here than on the grasslands, cheetahs have been able to survive in this semidesert. The other large population lives in the large Serengeti National Park in the East African nations of Kenya and Tanzania.

Chapter 2

The Hunt

The most important thing a cheetah must do to succeed at hunting is to take control of a hunting territory. Cheetahs need a great deal of room in order to hunt. The more cheetahs there are crowding a particular area, the more difficult it is for all of them to find food. For that reason, cheetahs stay away from one another. They establish the boundaries of their territory just as other cats do, by leaving their scent on rocks, trees, and other features of the land. As they roam across their territory, cheetahs sniff many of these same areas to see if intruders have left their scent.

Females may share territory with other cheetahs, although they will have nothing to do with them. Males often fight other cheetahs for the right to a certain territory. They may join forces with another cheetah to help them win fights for that territory. About two-thirds of the males in the Serengeti National Park live in pairs or trios. Some males never do win territory and have to wander hundreds of miles from their birthplace. Survival is very difficult for these homeless cheetahs.

Since cheetahs rely on their eyesight to find prey, they will take advantage of any opportunity to get a better look at their surroundings.

Daytime Hunters

Cheetahs are one of the few larger cats that hunt only in broad daylight. They rely on eyesight, rather than smell, to find their prey. They also need daylight to see where they are going and to watch for obstacles during their chase. Even a cat's keen night vision cannot warn them of rocks or holes in the ground while running at sixty miles per hour.

Cheetahs like to hunt during the late morning and early afternoon hours when more powerful predators such as lions are resting in the shade. While they, too, would rather sit out the heat of the noontime sun in the comfort of shade, cheetahs never pass up a kill if the chance arises. Even when they lie down to rest, they choose a spot that offers at least one good field of view. Periodically they wake themselves from their naps to check if a prey animal has wandered within range.

A cheetah begins its hunt by scouting the terrain for prey. Since they are taller than other large cats and have eyes located high on their heads, they can see a long ways. Often they gain a better look at their surroundings by climbing up on a termite mound, rock, low tree branch, or even the hood of a safari van.

Given a choice, cheetahs prefer to hunt wild prey rather than livestock. They are not large enough to pose a danger to adult cattle. Because they are so timid, they do not attack even goats and sheep in areas where the flocks are closely tended. There is no such thing as a man-eating cheetah. A single unarmed human or a dog can almost always frighten them away. But when prey is scarce and cheetahs go hungry, they will not pass up a chance to kill a sheep, goat, or an unprotected calf.

Stalking the Prey

Although they can run faster than all other animals, cheetahs cannot simply chase down every prey they see. They are sprinters that can run fast for only three hundred to six hundred yards before they tire. As long as it keeps at a

A cheetah freezes in place to avoid detection. A cheetah will remain motionless for a long time waiting to attack.

safe distance, a fast animal such as a Thomson's gazelle can easily avoid the predator. A cheetah's only chance for a kill is to creep within striking range before it is detected.

Their speed does give them an advantage, though, because cheetahs do not have to get as close to their prey as other large cats. Even when hunting the speediest gazelle, a cheetah needs only to approach to within thirty yards to have a good chance of success. By comparison, a lion must get much closer to its prey before pouncing in order to have a good chance at making a kill.

When it spots its prey, a cheetah crouches low. Keeping its eyes glued to the prey, it advances slowly through the long grass. Its spotted coat blends in well with the grass. This makes the cheetah hard to see as it crawls, and nearly impossible to detect when it stands still.

Gazelles are usually alert for signs of danger. When they raise their heads and look around, the cheetah freezes. It will not move again until the gazelles go back to their feeding.

Patience

As it draws closer to the gazelles, the cheetah's pace slows even further. Patience is the key to a successful hunt. The closer the cheetah can advance to its prey undetected, the greater the chance it will have a meal. Often a gazelle will sense the cheetah's presence, either through sight, smell, or warning from other animals. This does not mean that the cheetah will give up the hunt. It may remain still for a long time, as if waiting for the prey to forget about it.

The patience that the adult cheetah shows takes years to learn. Young cheetahs usually show poor judgment in their first hunting attempts. Instead of waiting for the right prey animal, they go after animals that are too large and strong for them to catch. They spoil their ambush by moving too carelessly or by not crouching low enough. Eager to bring down their prey, they often attack before they are close enough.

A cub learns to hunt by watching and practicing with its mother.

While the young cheetahs are learning to hunt, they make life very difficult for the mother. At about six months, the cubs chase after the mother as she stalks her prey. They spoil hunt after hunt with their noisy activity. As the cubs grow larger, they need much more food. Yet they are not able to make their own kills. This forces the mother to spend even more of her time hunting.

Closing In

As it waits in ambush, the cheetah singles out one animal. Once it chooses a victim, it pays no attention to any other prey. It will either kill this one or none at all on this hunt.

Sometimes, in very flat, open land, cheetahs will trot toward a large group of gazelles. In the confusion of the scattering herd, they may get close enough to make a kill without stalking. But even when approaching a large herd, cheetahs never chase a group of prey animals. They always single out one victim. Cheetahs will run right past other prey individuals without noticing them as they chase their chosen victim. If they fail to catch it, they break off the hunt rather than switch to a different individual.

The success of the hunt depends on the cheetah's judgment in selecting the right prey animal. In cases where the cheetah approaches a large herd, this means making an instant decision at the moment of attack. To avoid wasting time and

A cheetah walks by a herd of gazelles. Soon it will pick a victim and charge.

energy in unsuccessful high-speed chases, it goes after animals that are easiest to catch and kill. This often means young or very old animals.

The cheetah is especially watchful for careless prey. Sometimes a grazing gazelle will roam a few yards away from the others. It may even wander directly toward the cheetah. When this happens, the cheetah crouches even lower to the ground. As long as the gazelles are coming its way, it will not move again until the moment of attack.

A cheetah does not always attack when it comes within thirty yards of its prey. It knows that every step closer increases the odds that it will catch these very fast prey animals. It will inch closer and closer. When it gets as close as it possibly can without being seen, the predator prepares to spring.

Chapter 3

The Kill

Young cheetahs prepare their whole lives for the chase that follows a stalk. As young cubs, they often chase birds. As they grow older, they practice their running skills by teasing other animals. They even pester animals as large as a rhinoceros, and then easily dash away when the frustrated beast comes after them.

Cheetahs' instinct to chase prey is so strong that they are confused when a prey animal does not run away. Wildlife experts saw one case in which a gazelle had been badly wounded by a poacher. When charged by a cheetah, it struggled to gain its feet but was too weak to stand. Although the cheetah was hungry, it did not attack the animal. The cheetah stayed for an hour, waiting for the wounded beast to flee. Finally, it gave up and went off to search for a different prey. Cheetahs have also been known to give up a hunt in the rare cases when a prey animal stands its ground.

Cheetahs make an exception to this rule, however, in the case of fawns. A baby Thomson's gazelle will often drop to the ground and hide when danger approaches. Cheetahs appear to understand this behavior. They often search carefully in the grass where they have seen gazelles feeding, in hopes of turning up a hidden fawn.

The Chase

A cheetah begins its attack on a prey animal by rushing out of its hiding place. Startled out of its wits, the gazelle springs straight up in the air. Almost before it lands, it bolts in the opposite direction. The cheetah sprints after it so quickly that its legs become a blur.

The gazelle darts left and right. It stops and changes direction. Sometimes this action is enough to save the gazelle's life. With the balancing aid of its long tail, cheetahs are experts at making high-speed adjustments to stay with the prey. But as in any high-speed chase, the slightest slip of a foot can send an animal tumbling out of control. People have seen sprinting cheetahs lose their balance and take a hard fall when trying to react to a

Even though cheetahs can run faster than gazelles, gazelles can sometimes get away by zigzagging until the cheetah trips and falls or gets tired.

gazelle's move. Sloping or uneven ground is especially difficult for keeping balance.

If the cheetah is a split second off in matching any of the sharp turns of the gazelle, it loses ground. This makes the chase last longer. The gazelle needs only to avoid the predator for fifteen to twenty seconds before the cheetah tires and gives up.

The Kill

One reason why cheetahs like to attack only fleeing animals has to do with their method of killing. Cheetahs lack the strength and the powerful claws of other large cats. They are unable to pounce on an animal and wrestle it to the ground the way lions and tigers do. Instead, cheetahs bring down their prey with a swipe of the paw that trips the fleeing animal. They have a small claw on their forepaws, known as a dew claw, that helps hook the hind legs of their victim to knock it off balance. Since it is very difficult to trip an animal that is standing still, cheetahs are likely to leave them alone. Fawns are the exception because they are small and weak enough for a cheetah to overpower.

Like almost all large cats, cheetahs kill a fallen prey by going for the throat. Here again, though, cheetahs pay a price for their speed. The large nasal cavity that brings in extra oxygen for running leaves less room in the skull for teeth. Compared to other large cats, cheetahs have small, weak

Cheetahs kill their prey by biting and holding on to its throat until it suffocates.

jaws and smaller teeth for killing and eating their prey. They are not able to kill with a single well-placed bite as lions and tigers often do. The cheetah clamps its jaws over the throat of the prey and suffocates it, taking care to avoid the flailing hooves.

Because its jaws are not nearly as powerful as those of other large cats, the cheetah's kill may take several minutes. Even an animal as small as a gazelle will sometimes wriggle out of the grip of the predator and make its escape.

Learning to Kill

Cheetahs do not have the same instinct for killing that they have for chasing. At about six months, the cubs begin a long and often awkward training period in which they learn to capture their own food. When mothers capture small prey, such as a rabbit or fawn, they often bring it to the cubs and release it so that they may practice making the kill.

One scientist watched a litter of cubs the first time the mother brought them a still-living baby gazelle. At first, the cubs appeared confused as to what they were supposed to do. They flinched and ran away whenever the wounded gazelle kicked, trying to gain its feet.

If the captured prey is healthy enough to run, the young cheetahs instinctively chase after it. They swipe at it with their paws, trying to knock it down. Young cheetahs sometimes fail to bring down even small fawns. Even when they do, they

These cheetah cubs work together to try and catch a gazelle.

often have trouble hanging on or applying enough pressure to kill the animal. If the gazelle escapes from them, the mother recaptures it and brings it back to the cubs for another try. She will step in and make the kill herself only after giving the cubs many chances.

Successful Hunters

Because of their speed, cheetahs are more successful than other large cats at killing their prey. Lions, for example, seldom succeed on more than one of every three or four hunts. Tigers, despite their great strength, stealth, and leaping ability, fail on at least nine out of ten hunting efforts. Cheetahs, in contrast, are able to capture their prey nearly half of the time. When their target is a fawn or a hare, they almost always succeed.

Such a high success rate is a matter of life and death to a cheetah. Unlike lions, which are powerful enough to bring down wildebeests, zebras, and water buffalo that weigh over a thousand pounds, cheetahs have trouble killing animals that weigh over a hundred pounds. This means they must kill far more often than other

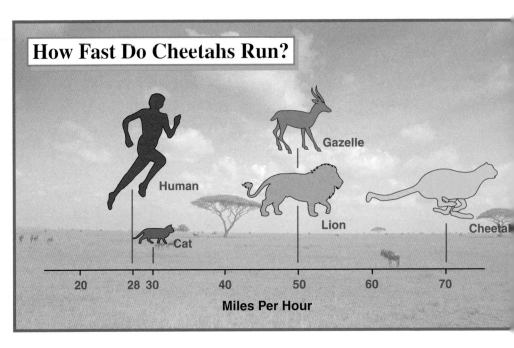

How Fast Do Cheetahs Run?

Human
Gazelle
Cat
Lion
Cheetah

20   28 30   40   50   60   70

Miles Per Hour

large cats in order to get enough meat to survive. For example, a lion may have to make only twenty to thirty kills a year to survive. A mother cheetah with a large family of cubs, however, cannot last more than a couple of days without making a kill. One mother tracked by researchers in the Serengeti killed twenty-four gazelles and a hare in twenty-six days.

Eating What They Kill

Cheetahs require a huge amount of energy for their hunts. Their furious sprint acceleration leaves their muscle cells starved for oxygen. Unfortunately for cheetahs, their method of killing does not allow them to quickly regain their oxygen supply. They have to use their mouths for strangling their prey. This means that when they need air the most, they must go several minutes breathing only through their nostrils. Although cheetahs' wide nasal passages allow them to take in more air through the nose than other cats, they are still extremely winded when they finish most kills.

Not only are cheetahs often exhausted after their high-speed chases, but they frequently overheat. This is especially true when hunting under the hot African sun. Overheated cheetahs may have to breathe as often as three and a half times per second as they attempt to cool off.

Many times cheetahs are unable to eat until they have had a chance to rest and cool down.

This cheetah drags its kill to a hiding place where it will rest and cool down before eating.

Sometimes they have enough energy left to drag their prey to a hiding place before they rest. Sometimes they must take time to recover before they can hide the food. This recovery period may last as long as a half hour. During that time, they can do little to protect their kill from scavengers such as lions and hyenas.

When cheetahs eat, they do so quickly and nervously. They constantly glance around, on the lookout for scavengers. They can eat a large amount of meat at a single feeding—up to a third of their body weight. The cheetah's habit of eating big meals makes it possible for wildlife experts to tell by a quick glance at the animal's stomach when it has last eaten.

Cheetahs do not save anything for future meals. Whatever they do not eat immediately upon killing, they leave for the other scavengers of the plain.

Cheetahs always have to be on the lookout for scavengers such as lions and hyenas who might steal their meal.

Chapter 4

The Hunter Becomes the Hunted

Cheetahs are not fighters by nature. Their usual reaction when they see a lion or leopard is to slink away with their head low. When any animal close to their size approaches them, they almost always run away.

All other meat eaters of the plains are aware of this weakness, and they keep a close watch for cheetahs. Some of them even follow cheetahs around in hopes of stealing a freshly killed meal from them. An example of the problem this causes for cheetahs was reported by a biologist who watched a female ambush and catch a Thomson's gazelle. Before she had even finished suffocating her prey, a hyena charged at her. The cheetah let go of the gazelle and retreated. The hyena snatched the dazed gazelle before it could start running and carried it away.

Lions and hyenas are the most common thieves of cheetah kills. Leopards and baboons will also move in when they get the chance. Cheetahs give up their kill to these animals without a fight. Even smaller animals such as jackals, warthogs, and vultures have been known to drive a tired cheetah away from its kill with little effort.

A Dangerous World

Adult cheetahs are too fast for large predators to catch, unless they are injured or surprised. In fact, more adult cheetahs are killed in fights with other cheetahs than by predators.

For cheetah cubs, however, the world is a very dangerous place. They are tiny, weighing only between five and ten ounces at birth. Baby cheetahs are utterly helpless and are easy prey for any predator that happens upon them. They are not able to open their eyes for the first week or so. They cannot even stand until about nine days. For the first three weeks, they are unable to crawl, much less run. This makes them easy prey for any predators that happen upon them.

During this time, a cheetah cub's only defense is its coat. The fur is not a golden brown coat with black spots like that of adult cheetahs. Instead, it has long, woolly, dirty white hair (called a

Baby cheetahs' eyes remain closed for about a week after birth. They will begin crawling after about three weeks.

mantle) that runs along its back and smoky gray hair on its underside.

This unusual coat looks very much like that of the honey badger. Honey badgers are tough, fierce little animals with sharp claws. Most predators learn to stay away from them and look for an easier meal. Many experts believe the baby cheetah's coat may serve to fool predators into thinking cheetah cubs are honey badgers and should be left alone. At three months, cheetahs lose their baby coats and spots begin to appear.

On the Move

Mother cheetahs are not able to offer their cubs much protection. Unlike other cats, they do not build a nest or burrow into a rocky den for shelter. The best they can do is hide the newborn cubs in tall grass, weeds, under bushes, or among rocks.

For much of the time that the cubs are in the lair, the mother must leave them alone. Even while the cubs feed on the mother's milk, the mother must keep hunting for her meat. This forces cheetah mothers to leave their young for long periods. When prey is scarce, the mother may not return for as long as forty-eight hours. In addition, there are times when the mother is worn out by the constant demands of the cubs and goes off by herself for a brief time to rest.

The mother cheetah does her best to protect the cubs by hiding them. Every few days, she moves the cubs to a different spot so that their scent will not build up in one spot and attract predators. Wildlife experts watched one mother cheetah move to ten different lairs in fifteen days. Sometimes the new lair is far away. Other times it may be as close as fifteen feet and may offer no more shelter than the abandoned one.

When her cubs are too young to crawl or walk, the mother picks them up one at a time by the scruff of the neck and carries them to the new spot. After carrying the last cub to the new location, the mother often returns to the original lair and searches briefly, as if checking to make sure she has not lost count and left one behind.

This constant moving continues after the cubs are able to walk by themselves. After the first five or six weeks, the cubs' diet changes from mother's milk to meat. They follow their mother around and begin eating from her kills. Since the cubs are not yet strong enough to travel long distances, the mother moves the lairs closer to the prime hunting

At six weeks of age, cheetah cubs begin sharing their mother's kills.

grounds. The bright white tip of the mother's tail serves as a marker to help the young keep sight of her as she walks through the tall grass. The cubs constantly chirp whenever the mother is out of sight in order to keep contact with her. She sometimes chirps back to help them locate her.

Personality Change

While cheetahs are normally timid, the mother may undergo a huge personality change when cubs are involved. Observers reported one case in which a lioness approached a cheetah and her two cubs. The mother cheetah growled a warning. Frightened out of their wits, the cubs started running. But, having no idea of what they were supposed to be running from, they ran straight toward the lioness.

The mother took a bold risk to save their lives. She outran the cubs to the lioness and swatted it with her forepaw. The lioness was so stunned by the cheetah's unexpected attack that she retreated. The cheetah chased her for about ten yards while the cubs scattered and dove for cover in the grass. Sometimes, the mother will purposely get lions to chase her in order to lead them away from her cubs.

Grim Facts

Lions and hyenas are by far the deadliest enemies of young cheetahs. Lions do not eat cheetahs, but will kill any that they find. Hyenas will make a meal of the cubs. Between them, they kill more than half of all cheetah cubs in the wild. Karen Laurenson made a study of cheetah cubs in the Serengeti. By placing radio collars on females, she was able to locate their lairs. While the females were away on hunts, she entered the lairs to count and weigh their newborn cubs. She found that by the time the cubs were old enough to leave the lair (about two months) only 36 of the 125 cubs were still alive. Only 6 of the cubs survived to become adults. Most experts put the death rate for wild cheetahs at 9 out of every 10. This compares with 5 out of 10 among young in other cats of the wild.

Cheetah numbers are not large even in game refuges that appear to offer ideal living conditions and unlimited prey. One reason for this is that the game reserves also provide protection for the cheetah's competitors. Even a huge park such as the Serengeti forces cheetahs to live close by lions and other natural enemies. The high numbers of lions and hyenas in such parks puts cheetah cubs at a terrible risk. It also increases the chances that a cheetah will lose its kill to a scavenger.

Human Enemies

Humans pose the greatest danger to adult cheetahs. Although few hunt them for their fur, many farmers believe cheetahs to be pests. Farmers have fenced in areas that had been open to wild grass-eating animals. This means that animals such as gazelles are unable to find food. As these animals disappear, cheetahs have more trouble finding food. Sometimes they kill livestock, which angers the farmers.

Cheetahs, especially the younger ones, are easy to trap and kill. Between 1980 and 1991, at least 6,800 cheetahs, more than a third of all wild cheetahs, were shot or sold off to zoos by ranchers. A few determined farmers can wipe out many cheetahs. In one recent year, two farmers destroyed thirty-nine cheetahs in Namibia.

Researchers place radio collars on cheetahs in order to track their movements and learn more about them.

Many wildlife groups have worked hard to protect cheetahs from humans and they have made progress. In most countries, shooting of cheetahs for sport is illegal. But, as wildlife experts point out, where protection is lacking, extinction remains a real possibility for the cheetah.

Zoo representatives visit an elementary class in Ohio to teach students about cheetahs and their struggle for survival.

Glossary

aardvark: A long-faced, long-eared animal of South Africa that feeds mainly on termites.

extinction: Complete and total disappearance of a species from the planet.

impala: A large, graceful antelope. They are the largest adult animals that cheetahs hunt.

jackal: A small, doglike animal of the African plains.

kudu: One of the largest antelopes. Only the males have horns. Cheetahs can bring down only the young.

lair: Resting place or home for wild animals and their young.

mantle: A furry coat that covers the back of a young cheetah.

poacher: A person who shoots animals when it is not legal.

retract: To pull back.

scavengers: Animals that eat prey killed by other animals.

scruff: Loose skin on the back of the neck.

springbok: A high-leaping antelope. At about sixty-five pounds, it is slightly larger than a Thomson's gazelle.

suffocate: To cut off the air supply of an animal so that it cannot breathe.

Thomson's gazelle: A small forty-pound antelope that is the favorite prey of cheetahs in those parts of Africa where it lives.

traction: The ability to get a good grip on the ground so that one does not slip when walking, running, or climbing.

wildebeest: Also known as a gnu, this large, cowlike antelope is less graceful than other antelope. They form circles to ward off the attacks of cheetahs.

For Further Exploration

David Alderton, *Wildcats of the World*. New York: Facts On File, 1993.

A little more challenging for young readers, this book contains plenty of information on the cheetah and its cousins in the wild.

Barbara Justin Esbensen, *Swift as the Wind*. New York: Orchard, 1996.

The stunning illustrations in this book help the young reader to get a good feel for the beauty and grace of the cheetah.

Shona Grimbly, *Endangered! Cheetah*. New York: Benchmark Books, 1999.

An easy-reading book that focuses on the dangers cheetahs face trying to survive in the modern world.

Barbara M. MacMillan, *Cheetahs*. Minneapolis: Carolrhoda, 1998.

An easy-reading, informative book with attractive illustrations.

Index

antelopes, 5

baboons, 35
blackbucks, 5
body, 6–7

cat family, 5–6
claws, 7, 9–10, 27
coats, 6, 35–36
cubs
    dangers to, 35
    food needs of, 22
    practice hunting, 21, 24,
        28–29

enemies
    animal 35, 39–40
    people, 40–41

food needs, 11–13, 22,
    32–33, 37

gazelles, 13, 20, 22, 23,
    24–26
grasslands, 15

habitat, 13, 15
heart, 10
herds, 22
honey badgers, 36–37

hunting
    habits
        ambushes, 20–21, 22,
            23
        attack, 22–23
        chase, 22–23, 24–25,
            28
        daytime, 18
        of mothers, 22, 37
        stalking, 19–20
    success, 30–31
    territory, 16–17
hyenas, 34–35, 39–40

injuries, 12

jaguars, 6

lairs, 37–39
Laurenson, Karen, 40
leopards, 6, 35
lions, 20, 28, 29, 30, 31, 35,
    39–40

mothers
    hunting by, 22
    hunting habits of, 37
    lairs and, 37–39

overheating, 31–32

oxygen needs, 11, 27, 31

personality, 39
plains, 13
population, 15
prey, 15, 18–19, 30
    blackbucks, 5
    gazelles, 13, 20, 22, 23,
        24–26
protection, 42

scavengers, 32, 33, 34–35
Serengeti National Park,
    13, 15, 17

size, 6
speed, 12–13
    balance and, 7–8, 25
    claws and, 7
    enemies and, 35
    stalking and, 20
strength, 9, 26–27

tail, 8, 25
teeth, 27–28
tigers, 28, 29–30

water needs, 13

Picture Credits